The Sacred Heart of Jesus

The Sacred Heart of Jesus
The Visual Evolution of a Devotion

David Morgan

AMSTERDAM UNIVERSITY PRESS

The Meertens Ethnology Cahiers are revised texts of the Meertens Ethnology Lectures. These lectures are presented by ground-breaking researchers in the field of ethnology and related disciplines at the Meertens Institute in Amsterdam, a research facility in language and culture in the Netherlands

The Meertens Institute is a research institute of the Royal Netherlands Academy of Arts and Sciences

Meertens Institute
Department of Ethnology
PO Box 94264
1090 GG Amsterdam
www.meertens.knaw.nl

Meertens Ethnology Cahier iv
Series Editor: Peter Jan Margry
peter.jan.margry@meertens.knaw.nl

Illustration front cover: Sacred heart of Jesus, coloured engraving of Currier & Ives, after 1856. Library of Congress.
Photo back cover: P.J. Margry

Cover design: Kok Korpershoek, Amsterdam
Lay out: JAPES, Amsterdam

ISBN   978 90 8964 019 2
ISSN   1872-0986

© Amsterdam University Press, 2008

All rights reserved. Without limiting the rights under copyright reserved above, no part of this book may be reproduced, stored in or introduced into a retrieval system, or transmitted, in any form or by any means (electronic, mechanical, photocopying, recording or otherwise) without the written permission of both the copyright owner and the author of the book.

From its modern inception in the seventeenth century to the present, the Sacred Heart of Jesus has been debated, promoted, and attacked from within as well as from without the Catholic Church. Images of the heart of Jesus vary considerably and correspond to shifting patterns of devotional practice as well as theological interpretation. Focusing on images and their uses, this essay will trace the history of the devotion among European and American Catholics.

1. Beginnings in Seventeenth-Century France

In a collection of her letters written over the last three or four years of her life, the French Visitationist nun, Margaret Mary Alacoque (1647-1690), reveals a great deal about the origin and meaning of her devotion to the Sacred Heart of Jesus. Opposition to the devotion arose in her own convent at Paray-le-Monial in the 1680s because it was a "new devotion." Because this charge was renewed by opponents of the devotion during the eighteenth and nineteenth centuries, the discourse that has long promoted Alacoque's cause has stressed the medieval and even apostolic origin of the Sacred Heart.[1] Although there were noteworthy influences on Alacoque from late medieval piety, the most characteristic features of her fervent dedication to the heart of Jesus were a product of eighteenth-century French spirituality, drawing for example from Frances de Sales, co-founder with Jeanne de Chantal of the Congregation of the Visitation of Holy Mary, or the Order of the Visitation in 1610, the order that Alacoque joined in 1671. In 1611 De Sales described in a letter to Chantal an image of a heart meant as an emblem for the new order. The heart anchored a cross that was inscribed with the names of Jesus and Mary. The heart was also pierced by two arrows and surrounded by a crown of thorns.[2]

The heart of Jesus and Mary was of central importance to another seventeenth-century French founder of a new religious order, Jean Eudes, who established the Congregation of Jesus and Mary in 1643, and in the same year created a liturgy to the Sacred Heart of Mary. Eudes described the heart of Jesus as a "furnace of ardent love," borrowing the words of St. Bernardine of Sienna.[3] Celebrating the tender intimacy of the hearts of Jesus and Mary, Eudes wrote: "With what flames of heavenly fire did the divine Heart of Jesus enkindle ever more and more the Virgin Heart of His most worthy Mother, especially when those two Hearts were so close to each other and so firmly united, while she bore Him in her womb, nursed Him, and held Him in her arms."[4]

But it was Alacoque who experienced the mystical revelation in which Jesus presented his heart to her on at two occasions. No less importantly, it was she who energetically launched the devotion, corresponding with several mothers superior in her order and with a number of sympathetic Jesuit priests, including her successive confessors. She enlisted all of them and the members of her own house in the cause, pressing them relentlessly to help her establish the devotion by authoring and circulating spiritual retreat manuals, devotional guides, and emblematic images of the Heart that appear to have originated in De Sales's image, but were soon modified to focus singularly on Jesus.

In June of 1675, as she contemplated the Blessed Sacrament, Alacoque experienced a vision in which Jesus displayed to her his heart. "Behold this Heart," he told her, "which has loved men so much... and in return I receive from the greater number nothing but ingratitude." Jesus asked Alacoque to set apart the Friday after the period of days each year devoted to celebrating the Feast of Corpus Christi (a medieval practice of adoring the body of Christ in the Sacrament of the Altar) "for a special Feast to honour My Heart."[5] Following this and other revelations over the next few years, Alacoque practiced especially debilitating forms of self-mortification in the fervent belief that Christ's reign in the soul was absolute: it depended on the complete vanquishing, even degradation, of the human self. Suffering became a pleasure, as she assured one correspondent, a fellow nun at another Visitationist convent: "There is no more suffering for those who ardently love the Sacred Heart of our lovable Jesus." To suffer was to draw close to the beloved: "Sorrow, humiliation, contempt, contradiction, everything most bitter to nature, is changed into love in this adorable Heart, which wishes to be loved most purely. He wishes to have all without reserve, He wishes to do everything in us without any resistance on our part. Let us surrender, then, to His power."[6] Alacoque's acts of self-mortification were staggering. Her superiors during the 1670s and 80s found her extreme regimen disturbing and challenging. She refused to eat or drink for weeks at a time and twice carved Jesus's name into her chest. Matters could become so grim that Alacoque came under direct order on several occasions to eat and regain her health.

The last seventeen years of her life, which became almost singularly devoted to the Sacred Heart, fall generally into three periods. Between 1673 and 1685 she struggled in the experience and then the interpretation of her revelation and ascetic response to the Sacred Heart's claim on her life. This period culminated in the completion of her *Autobiography*. Between 1685 and 1687 she became very occupied with the local, communal promotion of the cause, serving as director of novices, moving toward creating the communal practice of the devotion, and eventually seeing the devotion spread to several other convents, nurtured by Alacoque's extensive correspondence with nuns at Visitationist and Ursuline houses. From roughly 1688 to the end of her life, she consolidated her ideas in dialogue with Father Croiset, who produced an authoritative devotional guide dedicated to the Sacred Heart in 1691, the year following her death. In the last period of her career, Alacoque received an additional and dramatic revelation that set a new register for the devotion's expansion: Jesus disclosed that he wanted the King of France (Louis XIV) to consecrate himself and his entire court to the Sacred Heart. To the first phase belongs the core image as it was mystically revealed to Alacoque: the heart itself as it appeared to her "as a burning furnace," putting language to work that she no doubt found in Eudes's corpus of publications.[7] To the second phase, as she set up the heart's veneration among her fellow sisters, belongs the first fabrication of a pictorial image – simple engravings for display. And in the final phase comes the practice of painting the image for use on altars in chapels built especially in honor of the Sacred Heart.

In 1685, Alacoque was prepared to present her devotion in what she hoped would become coherent and communicable forms. She later told Croiset that when she'd been made director of nine or ten young novices, she had tried something new. On the Feast of her namesake, St. Margaret, in June of 1685, she asked the group to direct its veneration to the Sacred Heart:

> Having heard me speak of it, they were drawn with such ardor to honor this divine Heart, of Which I gave them a sketch traced on a little piece of paper with a pen, that they made great progress in perfection in a short time…They erected a little altar in His honor and tried to make reparation by their penances for the injuries and outrages committed against Him in the Blessed Sacrament.[8]

She went on to say that some of the novices procured money with which to make a painting of the Heart, but the mother superior forbade this "for fear they might be introducing a new devotion."[9] Public acts of devotion to a deceased person not yet recognized by the Church as worthy of veneration or any new practice of devotion to Jesus or the saints was forbidden without official sanction. Alacoque was forced, therefore, to practice her devotion to the Sacred Heart of Jesus in private. But she did not hesitate to share it with her colleagues, even encouraging them to join her. And it was in this zealous effort to establish the devotion that its visual forms came into play. She approved of several attempts at copying the image and worked with a donor to have the image reproduced as an engraving, to be made available for sale in groups of a dozen. Progress was very slow

Fig. 1. Engraving of Alacoque holding Sacred Heart drawing, after Savinien Petit; reproduced in *The Messenger of the Sacred Heart of Jesus* 25, no. 10 (October 1890), 720.

on this, but by the next year engravings of the Heart were in circulation. In a letter to Croiset in 1689, Alacoque described the image, which a nineteenth-century engraving pictures her holding up to the viewer (fig. 1):

> I saw this divine Heart as on a throne of flames, more brilliant than the sun and transparent as crystal. It had Its adorable wound and was encircled with a crown of thorns, which signified the pricks our sins caused Him. It was surmounted by a cross which signified

that, from the first moment of His Incarnation, that is, from the time this Sacred Heart was formed, the cross was planted in It...[10]

The emblematic nature of the image is clearly conveyed in this passage: elements of the image were understood to "signify" or convey meaning. For Alacoque, the visceral nature of the envisioned heart was not literally described by the image, as it would be later. At this earliest moment, the image was a device for promoting the devotion and serving as a focal point for altar and prayer. The real emphasis lay in the meaning coded in its features for prayer, meditation, and reparation.

The origin of the image that she mentioned appears uncertain. In her *Autobiography*, she referred to the image as a pen-and-ink sketch that she later remembered.[11] It seems likely that the image was one that portrayed what Francis de Sales had described, in which case it might very well have been an etching or engraving, having been produced by the Visitationist Order for use among the nuns. Or perhaps it was a sketch or a tracing of one such image. In any case, Alacoque does not say where it came from. But the image sprang to life in the close network of devotees in Visitationist houses. In a matter of a few months the image had proliferated, appearing in new versions at different convents whose residents were personally connected to Alacoque. Some of these sent her pictures of the Heart in the fall or winter of 1685, and painted and drawn versions spread during her remaining years.[12]

The sketch or print that she provided to the novices in the summer of 1685 appears to be the first one mentioned in her letters and autobiography.[13] But of greater significance than tracking the origin are the use and interpretation of the early imagery. On the basis of descriptions, it appears that all of the early images were emblematic in nature, like the one designed by De Sales, rather than physiological portrayals of a human heart, as the dominant iconography of the devotion would become in the next century. In a letter written in the second half of 1685, Alacoque stipulates the promises made by Jesus to those who honor his Sacred Heart, which includes an abundant shower of blessings "on every place where a picture of His divine Heart shall be set up and honored."[14] This was new and suggests that the turn to imagery was linked directly to the attempt, beginning in this year, to promote the devotion.

But the practice of visual display was not only, or even primarily, an attempt at advertising. The imagery was an engine of devotional piety, serving to focus and fan its energy. "I cannot help thinking," Alacoque wrote a mother superior in Moulins in the fall of 1686, "that the longing I felt to send you this picture of the Sacred Heart came from His desire to establish His kingdom in your community and His reign of love in our hearts."[15] In January of that year, Alacoque's former superior, Pérrone-Rosalie Greyfié, who had become superior at a Visitationist convent in Semur, sent Alacoque a new picture of the Sacred Heart, which had some differences from the one Alacoque had used the previous summer. Alacoque responded that she "took on a new life" when she saw the representation of the Heart. Receiving the image provided her great consolation, she said, because it signaled her colleague's willingness, "together with your whole community, to help us honor It."[16] The picture meant the expansion of the devotion beyond the private domain of Alacoque's convent. In a letter that spring, Alacoque described the new elements in the image from Greyfié, which served to underscore something key about all versions of the image at this time: "The four heads of Cherubim in the four corners, and the hearts intertwined in the crown of thorns. These latter represent those who love Him in suffering. The hearts that appear in the *liens d'amour* are those who love Him in joy."[17] The image was a coded symbol of community, symbolically imaging those engaged in the devotion, and was therefore suitable for placement on the altars that convents created for the new piety. As such, it marks a move beyond the core image of the flaming heart, wounded, topped by a cross, and surrounded by a crown of thorns, which Alacoque described in a letter to Croiset in 1689.[18]

Larger pictures of the Heart were placed on table-top altars, beside the crucifix, and in the final years of her life, on the altars of chapels; while small, paper versions were affixed by devotees to their person.[19]

A letter to Croiset indicates that the personal display was expressly commanded by Jesus as a public form of fulfilling his request for promoting the devotion, but also as a practice that resulted in special graces to the wearer. Alacoque anticipated an issue of great controversy in the next century when she described here the explicitly visceral nature of the heart image, also marking a new moment in the iconography – the shift from emblem to picture:

> It must be honored under the symbol of this Heart of flesh, Whose image He wished to be publicly exposed. He wanted me to carry it on my person, over my heart, that He might imprint His love there, fill my heart with all the gifts with which His own is filled, and destroy all inordinate affection. Wherever this sacred image would be exposed for veneration He would pour forth His graces and blessings.[20]

2. Critique and Defense in the Eighteenth Century

As the Counter-Reformation movement *par excellence*, the Society of Jesus set itself against the theological, liturgical, ecclesiastical, and metaphysical programs of the Protestant Reformers in order to champion the interests of the Catholic Church and to reverse the inroads made in northern Europe by Lutherans and Calvinists. In France, a principal target was the Huguenots, a Calvinist sect subjected to violent persecution by Cardinal Richelieu. Their persecution was continued after Richelieu's death by Louis XIV, who revoked the Edict of Nantes in 1685. Alacoque herself had cheered the effort to convert the Huguenots through the ministrations of the Sacred Heart and had blamed these "heretics" and "infidels" for the delay in securing an engraved image of the Sacred Heart for wide distribution when the priest engaged in the task was distracted by efforts among the Huguenots.[21] But reform was also pursued within the Catholic Church by proponents of Jansenism, which began with the eponymous Cornelius

Jansen's study of Augustine's theology, *Augustinus* (1640), and extended to the eve of the French Revolution.

Jansenism was a reform movement within the Church undertaken by intellectuals in the Netherlands, France, and Italy who followed Jansenius in a reading of Augustine that stressed a narrow understanding of salvation as divinely pre-determined. This meant that only a limited number of the elect were to be redeemed. God, the absolute sovereign, could not be swayed to change his mind by human efforts of penance or by the issuing of papal indulgences to induce penance among sinners. Grace was efficacious only among those elected or chosen by God to be saved. But the movement was not only theological in character. Jansenism translated into a remarkable politics of reform, whose significance is not measurable simply in terms of actual change, which was limited, but in impact on the establishment. The theology of efficacious grace espoused by Jansenism posed a direct threat to the spiritual economy controlled by the Papacy since Jansenism undermined the Office of the Keys (jurisdiction over spiritual matters resting with the pope) and the primacy of the bishop of Rome. Gallican sentiments in France welcomed Jansenist ideas whereas Ultramontanists in France and elsewhere, which included the Jesuit Order when it enjoyed the favor of the current pope, strongly opposed Jansenism.[22]

Devotion to the Sacred Heart appealed to the Jesuits (as well as to many others) because it took seriously the response of the devout to the sacrificial offering of grace by Jesus. Each person was called to struggle toward making amends, paying reparations of the damage to God caused by sin. This was to be done by penitential means, availing oneself of the Eucharist, undertaking *ex-voto* pledges such as pilgrimage, praying with the rosary, attending masses on feast days, displaying and contemplating the image of the Sacred Heart as well as images of saints, Jesus, and Mary, and through the acquisition of indulgences issued by popes and bishops in connection with the adoration of the Host, feast days, pilgrimage, or various novenas or other devotional practices. All of these served as the means for repaying the honor taken from God by human sin. All served as forms of delivering grace, blessing, and spiritual favors to the practitioner. All were regarded as the individual's response to the offer of forgiveness.

This was enough for the Jansenists to object to, but there was more. As one scholar aptly put it: "The contrast between this baroque spirituality and Jansenist austerity could not have been stronger."[23] In 1726 Joseph de Gallifet, postulator to the Sacred Congregation of Rites of the case for honoring the Sacred Heart of Jesus with a universal feast, published his lengthy argument in Latin. In 1733 he issued an expanded edition in French, which continued to expand in several editions.[24] Gallifet's book promoted the Baroque sensuousness of Alacoque's passionate devotion and mystical visions. Her experience of the Sacred Heart celebrated a material penitentialism as a necessary aspect of the task of reparations. Gallifet stressed the power of the Sacred Heart as a refuge from the anger of God. The Sacred Heart was, as Alacoque had said, a "second mediator," the divine means of curbing the righteous impulse to retribution.[25] A case in point for Gallifet was the remission of the plague in Marseilles in 1720 after the bishop of Marseilles had publicly consecrated himself to the Sacred Heart. As Gallifet put it, the bishop succeeded in "warding off the divine vengeance" deserved by sin. In fact, Gallifet even suggested that God had sent the plague in order "to secure glory for the Heart of His Son."[26] This raises the possibility that a powerful appeal of the Sacred Heart was theodicy: God slaughtered himself for the sake of placating his wrathful need to punish humanity. The Sacred Heart is the evidence of divine self-sacrifice. This intensified theological stature of the devotion contributed to the most controversial aspect of it: the visceral heart. It was necessary to show the heart as carnal, Gallifet said, "in the simple and natural sense, and not metaphorically," in order to present the visual evidence of the atoning holocaust.[27] Human suffering's embodied nature was met and affirmed in the dissected viscera of Jesus. Reparations were powerfully repaid through devotion to the Heart, and the issuing of indulgences by bishops and popes, beginning as early as 1692, just two years after Alacoque's death, assured the currency of the devotion in the spiritual economy of compensating God for the debt of sin.

Fig. 2. Pompeo Batoni, "The Sacred Heart of Jesus", 1767, oil on copper, Il Gesu, Rome.

During Alacoque's lifetime the heart was visualized only as an emblem. But the visceral nature of the heart in her devotion was fundamental. The promoters of the devotion over the next decades steadfastly resisted softening the commitment to the fleshy organ, even laying the groundwork for new iconography that would celebrate the heart as organ. Instead of the highly emblematic imagery of the heart conceived by De Sales and Alacoque in the previous century, the seventeenth-century saw the new imagery fix on the heart in relation to the person of Jesus, often in direct response to criticism from opponents of the devotion. Gallifet stressed the importance of the heart as material organ and seat of the affections and person. It was a point that met significant resistance in the official assessment of the devotion's cause, ultimately resulting in the Congregation of Sacred Rites' decision in 1726 against establishing a universal feast in honor of the Sacred Heart. It was a strategic error for which later proponents continued to blame Gallifet. In the introduction to his *Novena to the Sacred Heart* (1758), Alphonsus de Liguori faulted Gallifet for arguing that "all the sentiments of the soul could be said to have their source in the heart and not in the head."[28] Liguori hoped, nevertheless, that the Church would recognize the devotion. In 1765, Clement XIII did so by approving a liturgical feast of the Sacred Heart.

The intimacy with which devotees practiced the devotion is registered in the new iconography that emerged quickly following the Vatican's official recognition. Art historian Jon Seydl has argued very perceptively that what came to be the most important and enduring portrayal of the Sacred Heart, painted in 1767 by the Italian artist Pompeo Batoni for placement on an altar in the Church of the Gesu in Rome (fig. 2), did not operate by telling the story of the revelation, but of showing the event itself in a way that "engages the beholder in a deeply personal exchange that stands outside space and time. Christ's outward gaze, locking eyes with the beholder, cements this relationship."[29] As Seydl shows, critics objected to the separation of the heart from the body of Jesus in Alacoque's visions and in the devotional practice because it sundered the incarnation's unity of body and Word, the second person of the Trinity.[30] Batoni's image may be read as replying to the criticism of the devotion by assuring viewers of the Sacred Heart's integration of the two: Jesus serenely holds his own heart, gesturing to it in order to affirm its essential unity with his life, body, mission, and Trinitarian nature. New to the cult image is the penetrating gaze of the figure, now understood as a portrait that seeks out the viewer's eye for an intimate connection, as if the image pleads for a personal and thoroughgoing response from those who look at it. The gaze of Christ introduces his person, the mysterious presence of the Godhead in the incarnate Messiah, countering the claim that the devotion separated the two natures of the God-Man. The portrait also safeguarded the fleshy organ for the devotion, whose materiality mattered keenly to popular adherence.

If there were any doubt about that, an Italian mob settled the matter. In 1787, riotous crowds in Prato trashed the palace of Bishop Scipio de Ricci in response to his efforts at Jansenist reform, which included criticizing the devotion to the Sacred Heart, reducing the number of altars in churches to one, removing excessive images and reliquaries, placing relics within the altar, out of sight, and demoting the use of indulgences.[31] To the people and to Ricci's many Jesuit detractors, such efforts spelled Calvinism.[32] Bishop of Pistoia and Prato in Tuscany, Ricci corresponded extensively with French Jansenists, translated and published their works as tracts in Italian, and waged a long battle over the supremacy of the Papacy versus the primacy of bishops, the separation of ecclesiastical and state power, educational reform for clergy, the subordination of religious orders to the bishop, and the strict regulation of devotional life, including the use of relics, indulgences, and images. Ricci advocated a model of governance that secular courts enthusiastically embraced because he argued for the freedom of civil power from ecclesiastical control. As bishop (from 1780 to 1795, when he was forced to resign), he operated with the blessing of his sovereign, Peter Leopold, Grand Duke of Tuscany, who followed his brother, Joseph II, ruler of Austria, in seeking to institute liberal ecclesiastical reforms that subordinated the Church to civil authority.

In the summer of 1781, one year after being consecrated as a bishop, Ricci inaugurated a robust career of theological publications by issuing a pastoral letter entitled "On the New Devotion to the Heart of Jesus." "In the effete times in which we live," it began, "we have only too many devotions... Christians have made themselves a laughing stock to unbelievers by their mass of fantastical, womanish, and ridiculous devotions." Ricci argued that efforts to establish the feast of the Sacred Heart had been resisted by many theologians in Rome "who rejected the many booklets and the offensive pictures of the propagandists" that promoted the cause. If, he reasoned with his readers, "the object of your adoration and delight is the Holy Sacrament of the Eucharist, where there is not only the Heart of Jesus Christ but the fullness of the Godhead in two natures, hypostatically united and truly present – in the words of St. Augustine, a *symbol of love*, a sacrament of unity... what need have you to take on a new devotion to the Sacred Heart of Jesus, without which for all these centuries past the true Faithful attained the highest degree of sanctity?"[33] The "womanish" practice of the devotion was certainly a reference to the passionate nature of Alacoque's mystical eroticism, but was no doubt also directed at the larger target of the tendency of penitential practices to appeal to the body in powerful ways. The riot in 1787 would be fomented in part by fear that Ricci had advocated removing the relic of the Virgin's belt from the Cathedral in Prato. Ricci wished to dismiss the appeal of the Sacred Heart as "new" and inessential. In a polemical discourse structured by binary opposites, the appropriately masculine form of faith adhered to the spiritual dimension of Christ present to faith as a "symbol of love."

In 1794, the same year in which he officially approved the devotion to the Sacred Heart and issued indulgences to those who practiced it, Pius VI issued a bull, *Auctorem Fidei*, condemning Jansenism and Ricci's principles. The points Pius made serve to highlight the anti-modern disposition of the establishment, which comports with the devotion to the Sacred Heart. The penitential economy to which images were closely associated in medieval no less than Baroque Catholic piety turned on indulgences. Just as Luther had criticized them, launching the Protestant Reformation in 1517, Ricci sought to reign in the definition and practice of indulgences, which were a singular aspect of the Church's power in the operation of the Office of the Keys, that is, managing the forgiveness of sins. Ricci argued that an indulgence was actually no more than "that part of the penance which had been established by the canons for the sinner," that is, the lenience the Church may show toward the sinner is not forgiving the sin itself, but forgoing the penitential procedure levied on the sinner to achieve forgiveness from God. Pius condemned the claim as "false, rash, injurious to the merits of Christ, [and] already condemned in article 19 of Luther."[34] Ricci likewise rejected the late medieval idea on which indulgences were based: "The poorly understood treasury of the merits of Christ and of the saints," which amounted to the heavenly repository of spiritual capital on which indulgences drew.[35] To Ricci's claim that by worshipping the Heart of Jesus, devotees distinguished it from the divinity, making the material flesh the object of worship, Pius countered that "when they worship the Heart of Jesus it is, namely, the heart of the person of the Word, with whom it has been inseparably united."[36]

3. Proliferation of the New Iconography in Nineteenth-Century France and America

Ricci lost the battle against the Sacred Heart and the larger economy of penitentialism. But the career of the devotion in the nineteenth century underwent important institutional and social changes that are registered in its visual representation. The Daughters of the Sacred Heart, founded and led by Sophie Barat (1779-1865), invested the devotion in an order committed to teaching children, largely the children of France's aristocracy. The growth of convent schools in the order was dramatic. Founded in 1800, by 1829 the order numbered 24 houses. A decade later it boasted 40. By 1844 it had added 17 more. In the year of Barat's death, the number had risen to 86 houses, stretching from France to the United States.[37] As a result, a more pastoral and didactic temperament characterized the devotion. Although Barat remained committed to Alacoque's ideal of the forgetting of self, the ascetic extreme was replaced by an ethic of service and self-sacrifice in the order's mission of teaching. Barat's dedication to the cause made one former student observe: "She was truly a mother in the midst of her children… Our Mother General seemed like the image of Jesus Christ Himself, and of His adorable Heart."[38] In light of the very practical mission of the order, it follows that Barat balanced a mystical self-transcendence with a deeply committed concern for the wellbeing of others. She urged her sisters to take Alacoque as a model, "not in the extraordinary manifestations but in her obedience, charity, union with Jesus Christ, to the degree that each one can reach."[39]

Contemporary devotional guides on the Sacred Heart also helped turn an important corner. Peter Arnoudt, a Jesuit father, published a guide in 1846, *The Imitation of the Sacred Heart of Jesus*, in which Alacoque's erotic imagery was replaced by filial discipleship. Masochistic self-emptying was exchanged for pastoral calm and parental tenderness. The work is organized as a dialogue in which Jesus addresses a follower in characteristically affectionate words: "Come, My Child, take up My yoke upon thee; for My yoke is sweet, and My burden light. My service, Child, is not that of a tyrant, nor of a harsh master; but of a most loving Father, who is near His children, who are submissive to Him, that He may help and entertain them."[40] Rather than the soul's lover, Jesus was a gentle parent who offered refuge from the storms of life: "In My Heart thou shalt find peace and tranquility, which the world cannot give nor take away."[41]

Given this shift in sensibility, it is not surprising to find a corresponding change in the iconography of the Sacred Heart. When the Society moved to a new headquarters in Paris in November of 1858, the chapel of the mother house of the Daughters of the Sacred Heart, which was completed in the spring of the following year, featured "a full-length painting of the Sacred Heart over the altar."[42] Alacoque herself appeared with growing frequency in nineteenth-century iconography since portraying her person as in Fig. 1 or at key moments in her revelations suited the cause of her beatification as well as the international spread of the Daughters of the Sacred Heart. Batoni's eighteenth-century portrayal of Jesus bearing the Sacred Heart (see fig. 2) exerted broad influence and became virtually canonical during the second half of the nineteenth century, in part because of its enormous dissemination in mass-produced print media (figs. 3-4). Sometimes the images are only vaguely related to Batoni's, as in the case of Fig. 3. With other instances, however, the debt is unmistakable, as with Fig. 4, a lithograph produced in Boston, perhaps in 1856, when Pius IX proclaimed the Feast of the Sacred Heart universal; or in 1864, when he announced the beatification of Alacoque.[43] The inti-

Fig. 3. "Sacred Heart of Jesus", undated lithograph. Collection of the author.

Fig. 4. "The Sacred Heart of Jesus", mid-nineteenth century, lithograph printed by Thomas B. Noonan & Co., Boston. Courtesy Library of Congress.

mate portrait style, especially the direct gaze, appealed strongly to the mode of sympathy that developed in popular piety during the nineteenth century. The image appeared in inexpensive lithographic form as holy cards, posters and large prints for display in churches, schools, and homes.[44] In the year following Alacoque's beatification and over the next decade, many French dioceses consecrated themselves to the Sacred Heart. A poster created to celebrate the consecration of the diocese of Laval in 1865, produced as a hand-tinted lithograph by a firm in Épinal, shows a half-length image of Jesus, parting his mantle to display the glowing heart, very similar to Fig. 3 reproduced here.[45] Though critics often point out that this imagery seems excessively effeminate, the same quality is to be found in Batoni's archetype. The feminine character continued to appeal to devotees in part because of the way in which Mother Barat came to resemble Jesus for her students and admirers. Indeed, one imagines the appeal of the devotion to many women may have been the tenderness and accessibility, even vulnerability, of this Jesus, shown in the intimate act of exposing his heart to Alacoque, but more importantly to anyone endeared to his gentle, kindhearted attentions.

Of course, this reading should be balanced with the continued political career of the devotion in nineteenth-century France. Raymond Jonas has chronicled the history of the devotion to the Sacred Heart in France from Margaret-Mary Alacoque's life to the late nineteenth century.[46] During the Revolution, the Sacred Heart was the emblem of the monarchy, serving as insignia among devotees and as the despised symbol of reaction fought by the Republicans. As another historian of the Sacred Heart put it, during the period of the Revolution: "The image of the heart of Jesus became a suspect sign, a religious symbol, a political symbol; to wear it was not an act of devotion but to declare oneself an un-sworn priest, aristocrat, counter-revolutionary."[47] The image of the Sacred Heart continued to be associated with the monarchy during the Restoration and was championed by the Church in opposition to republican forces through the period of the Commune. French volunteers who fought on behalf of the embattled papacy against Italian Republicans followed eighteenth-century practice and sewed cloth images of the Sacred Heart to their uniforms. French devotion to the Sacred Heart culminated in the construction of the Basilique du Sacré-Coeur de Jésus de Montmartre in the 1880s. Jonas examines the remarkable tradition among royalist French Catholics of interpreting republican revolution as a divine scourge unleashed on the nation as punishment for its errant ways. National consecration to the Sacred Heart was the proper means of making penance and securing divine forgiveness.[48]

Yet the history on which I wish to focus is the visual aspect, which plays a smaller role in Jonas's account. In the course of the nineteenth century, a new iconographical tradition of the Sacred Heart developed in France. The heart was placed in the midst of the chest of Jesus, who was shown opening his tunic to reveal the flaming organ. The disclosure reenacts the intimate revelation to Alacoque, in effect, sharing his heart with all believers. But it changed the way that people engaged with the Sacred Heart. It was no longer a bloody device signaling penitential suffering, but a gentle, inviting portrait of a benign savior who welcomed an intimate relationship with the devotee, and in less visceral terms than Batoni's influential image. Neither the eroticism nor the excruciating penance of Alacoque were stressed by the popular nineteenth-century portrait of Jesus (fig. 3). The iconography changed to accommodate the different form of piety. Jesus tenderly offers himself, gazing softly but steadily into the eyes of viewers. Two variations appear in the nineteenth century: Jesus withdrawing his robe, cape, or tunic to show the radiant heart; and Jesus showing the stigmatum in his right hand and pointing to the heart with his left hand, which may also bear the stigmatum. Both instances reference the visions of Alacoque, in which Jesus associates the Sacred Heart with the Eucharist. These forms accommodated the piety practiced in the nineteenth-century convent and school, which welcomed an effeminate Jesus, who was thereby likened to those who sought out sympathy with him, i.e. primarily women and children. His lips are delicate and red, his eyes are large, demure, and blue. His head tilts slightly, giving his expression a familiarity. His fingers are long and attenuated, delicately terminating in carefully manicured nails. His body is concealed in a large, thick robe and tunic, which focuses the viewer's attention on the heart and the gaze.

The new image substitutes closeness and delicacy of feeling for the older passion, devoted personal relationship for penitential anguish. The point was to offer an interactive device: Jesus himself returns the gaze of the viewer, offering to suffer with the viewer, to feel her pain, to respond to her suffering and misery with his pastoral and comforting presence. The heart itself, disembodied and hovering as a bloody organ, was the emblem of Christ's suffering, into which the practitioner of Baroque visual piety was meant to vanish. Nineteenth-century devotional culture reversed the focus of the practice by situating the heart in or on the surface of Christ's body and subordinating the heart to the countenance of Jesus, who trains his sight on the viewer. Jesus was now able to respond to the viewer, to be the sympathetic soul who is like those devoted to him and therefore personally reassuring to them. Alacoque had to pay for intimacy with pain, emptying herself out in order to join the sacred lover, employing a visual piety of *empathy*. Modern devotees came to rely on a visual piety of *sympathy* in which likeness but not identity prevailed. Jesus was sympathetic toward his followers, which is visually signaled in his tenderness and androgyny.[49]

In 1874, the American convert to Catholicism, Orestes Brownson, expressed his discomfort with the "new devotion" and recalled Ricci's objection to the way in which it split the material organ from the hypostatic union of the God-Man. "We confess the picture," he wrote, "the model of which the Blessed Margaret Mary says she was shown by our Lord himself, strikes us not as a heart inflamed with love, but as a wounded and bleeding heart, and which repels rather than attracts us. It does not help our devotion."[50] Brownson's remarks did not go unnoticed. He was accused by one reader of raising objections "formerly urged by the Jansenists, and therefore are suggested by the enemy of God and man."[51] Another reader scolded Brownson for speaking "the very language of the Jansenists, those embittered enemies of the Devotion," and argued that "the Church wishes that her children should foster a particular devotion to the heart of flesh of

Jesus, but not in the carnal sense of the Jansenists and other adversaries of this devotion."[52]

The exchange in which Orestes Brownson became engaged during 1874 marks an important period in the emergence of a new regime in the visual representation of the devotion. Images of the Heart as a bodily organ co-existed with the new iconography of the Heart graphically imposed on the portrait of Jesus. Fig. 4 endorsed the unity of flesh and divinity in Batoni's pictorial formula of a frontal portrait of Jesus gazing directly into the viewer's eye, holding for the viewer's contemplation a robustly modeled organ, anatomically correct in size, bearing a prickly wreath of thorns and a wide gash. If that weren't enough, the other hand of Christ displays the nail wound, which Batoni's image lacks. Fig. 4 recycles the eighteenth-century format, but infuses it with even more orthodox and traditional notions of the devotion, as if to assert more stolidly than ever the corporeal nature of the heart. It is just the emphasis on the visceral organ that Brownson and like-minded Catholics found repulsive. But clearly not all Catholics, as a "Hymn of Reparation" printed in an 1875 issue of *The Messenger of the Sacred Heart* demonstrates:

> Upon the altar night and day
>   The Heart of Jesus lies,
> And night and day throughout the world
>   Do men its claims despise;
> For by their cold, ungrateful lives,
>   They pierce It through and through:
> And by the scourges of their crimes,
>   Its agonies renew.[53]

This was the material tissue that Jesus presents in Fig. 4, displaying so prominently the wound he endured for the sins that continue to require the reparation intoned by the hymn. But at the same time the devotion was metamorphosed by poetry and imagery that presented the heart as an icon, as a lens through which the devout are enjoined to look in order to see the love that "informs" the heart.

In 1872, the American edition of *The Messenger of the Sacred Heart of Jesus* published the translation of a Dutch "Catechism of the Devotion to the Heart of Jesus" by a Jesuit priest, R. Pierik,[54] which seems to demote the materiality of the heart. Recognizing the twofold object of the devotion, "one visible and material, the other invisible and spiritual," Pierik's Catechism nevertheless lays by far the greater emphasis on the spiritual: "Both of these are united, but they have this peculiar to each, that the spiritual object communicates its own worth and merit to the material object, whilst it is the material object that lends its name to the particular devotion or feast in question."[55] This gives the material aspect of the Sacred Heart no more than a nominal role. The spiritual object of the devotion is the love of Jesus and the "final object" of the devotion is "Jesus Himself, His divine Person whom I honor when I honor His Heart."[56] The Catechism goes on to insist that the two, heart and person, are never to be separated, then poses a question that refers the respondent to the portrait of Jesus with the Sacred Heart: "When you look on any picture of Jesus showing to you His Divine Heart, can you represent to yourself all that here has been said?" The response is striking for its re-situation of the visual piety of the devotion:

> Readily. The Heart which He displays to me is the immediate, sensible, material object which I venerate. This Heart itself is an emblem of love, and this love, which is the spiritual object of my veneration, is besides represented to one by the flames which surround the Heart. In fine, the person who shoes it to me is Jesus, to whom reverts all the homage which is exhibited. I honor then Jesus Himself, for His love, in His Heart which is the furnace of that love.[57]

The next section of the Catechism asks the catechumen to look upon the picture once again and provide an overview of all the meanings of the devotion as they are encoded in its features. The passage is important for the list of emblematic interpretations it offers, indicating that the image is a kind of lexicon of visual codes:

The Heart which Jesus presents to me recalls His love, which naturally demands that I should love Him. The flames which surround the Heart speak to me again of His infinite love, which the Eucharist [sic] reveals to me. The Cross, the crown of thorns, the gaping wound of the Heart – of what do they speak to me but of His cruel Passion and bitter sufferings? And if I notice Jesus' gaze fixed upon me, His right hand, which seemed to ask for my heart, do I not hear the words, *"Learn of Me, for I am meek and humble of heart. Follow me?"*[58]

If it were not clear from this litany of explanations, the catechism once again returns to the symbolic nature of the image by asking "What do you understand by an emblem?" The reply draws a firm distinction between sign and referent: "An image which speaks to the senses; that is to say, a thing or the representation of a thing which, appearing materially to our eyes, recalls to our minds an immaterial, spiritual thing different from the first. Thus, for instance, a heart, or the picture of a heart, is the emblem of love."[59] The Catechism went on to break down the parts of the image and explicate each of them further. But as abstract as the components become, encoded with a theology that remains quite mystical and sensuous, at least in its origins, the image of Jesus itself is nevertheless imbued with a presence that is quite interactive, as the catechumen's reply suggests: "Jesus' gaze fixed upon me" seems to bid the viewer's heart to emulate his meekness. A host of indulgences outlined by the Catechism offer good reason to do so. And Jesus is said to have promised through Alacoque that he "will bless the dwellings where the Image of My Sacred Heart shall be exposed and honored."[60] The Catechism quietly morphed Alacoque's adored Heart into the portrait of Jesus that returns the viewer's gaze. The Boston print holds both visual features in balance – the corporeal organ and the direct gaze. Placing the corporeal heart on or in the chest, Fig. 3 balances it with the direct gaze of Jesus's eyes. This portrait-type would remain much more popular and widespread as an image than Fig. 4.

The aim was to integrate the heart into the person of Jesus in a way that invited a personal response. An article entitled "Sympathy with Jesus," translated from a German edition of *The Messenger*, proclaimed that Catholics ought to desire "sympathy with Jesus" as a duty.[61] Mary and Joseph "deeply sympathized with Jesus," "they were compassionated toward Jesus," "they felt with Jesus," and they were "the true friends of Jesus."[62] To have sympathy with Jesus meant to respond to his suffering and humiliation as misfortunes occurring to one's friend or family member: "The first and the most essential point to be settled by every honest Christian is his own relations with Jesus Christ, that he must become acquainted with his interior state." In order to do that, each Christian must "examine whether he really sympathizes with his persecuted Jesus, whether he bears Him within his heart, whether he is firmly resolved on no consideration to close his heart against his Lord and Master."[63] An image that engages the pious viewer with a direct gaze, bringing the two parties together in an affective resonance, was better calculated to achieve that end than the image of the lone heart. The move from empathy to sympathy distanced viewers from Alacoque's experience, even if they were not aware of it. Alacoque held sympathy in low esteem. In a letter to a friend she regretted the sympathy shown her by colleagues over a painful cut in her finger: their expression to her of how much she must have been suffering "has given me a taste of how pleasing to nature it is to be sympathized with. Nature cannot bring itself to suffer humiliation, contempt, and abandonment by creatures without some support."[64]

In 1890, the *Messenger* ran a story about the Basilica of the Sacred Heart of Jesus nearly completed on Montmartre in Paris and included an illustration of a monumental statue of Jesus that was said to be in the basilica (fig. 5).[65] The statue as it appears in the engraving is noteworthy because it balances the tendencies noted so far: the fetishistic realism of Alacoque, the iconic portrait-type, and the symbolic treatment of the heart. The naturalistically rendered figure of Jesus contrasts with the small symbol inscribed on the drapery over his chest, yet the entire figure stands on what appears to be a gigantic heart,

Fig. 5. Statue of the Sacred Heart, engraving in *The Messenger of the Sacred Heart of Jesus* 25, no. 10 (October 1890), 732.

wrapped in the fervid mists of the fiery organ, to which are attached the implements of Christ's Passion. The design simultaneously affirms the Eucharistic significance of the Cross and Passion, the Lordship of the Sacred Heart, and the universal embrace of the love celebrated by the devotion. Christ gazes steadily at viewers, as if redirecting his look from the private vision of Alacoque to all of humankind. The mystic is replaced by the entire race, as Leo XIII would effect in his encyclical of 1899, "Annum Sacrum," consecrating the human race to the Sacred Heart.

Fig. 6. "Sacred Heart", Church of St. John, Baexem, Limburg, 1931.
Photo: E. Geelen.

4. Commemorative Statuary in Twentieth-Century Netherlands

A gradual symbolization of the Heart is discernible in the nineteenth and twentieth centuries which encodes it with remembered meanings rather than part of a portrait-icon, on the one hand, or a visceral floating organ of glistening tissue exuding flames, on the other. The discourse on the Heart as "symbol" goes back, as we have seen, to the Vatican's review of the devotion in the 1720s, and resounded in every debate and controversy about the devotion since. There is no reason, in fact, given the inherent tension between symbol and organ, why devotees can't affirm both aspects, and certainly that is what the catechists sought to achieve in their didactics. Yet we may see the symbolic aspect emerge to prominence during the twentieth century, at

Fig. 7. J. Thissen, Roermond, "I am King", Church of St. Joseph, Beringe, Limburg, 1938. Photo: E. Geelen.

least in certain kinds of representations of the Sacred Heart, and in some cases the heart has vanished altogether from portrayals of the Sacred Heart of Jesus.

A body of statuary of the Sacred Heart of Jesus erected in the region of Limburg largely from the 1920s through the 1940s, collected and studied by Godfried Egelie, documents the continuing development of the iconography and its corresponding meanings and uses.[66] The statues, carved in stone and placed on church, school or monastery grounds, serve a number of purposes. Some adorn gardens and meditative spaces for walks. In the majority of cases, the statues commemorate a priest or celebrate his retirement from the ministry, the anniversary of his priesthood, or the career of a pastor's service in the community. Families of nuns sometimes dedicate a statue on the occasion of the nun's taking vows. Others remember local individuals fallen in the first or second world war. Mayors and municipalities raise statues in honor of a parish or priest. In almost every case, the statues mark a public recognition of an individual or institution's service by affirming the sacrifice of and devotion to the Sacred Heart of Jesus. The gestures vary, but fall into a few clear categories (see figs. 6-7, 10): 1) arms outspread; 2) arms displaying palms, usually bearing wounds; and 3) hands configured in a gesture of benediction, teaching, or presentation of the heart.

The unmistakably pastoral purpose of the statues is doubly underscored by the gestures and the inscriptions. Quite typically, Jesus presents himself to the viewer, welcoming response (fig. 6). The most common inscription is some portion of his words in Matthew 11: 28 – "Come to me, all who labor and are heavy laden, and I will give you rest." Jesus has just told his listeners that he is the distinctive revelation of God and the portal through which access to the father is possible. He is himself the very revelation of the Godhead: "No one knows the Father except the Son and any one to whom the Son chooses to reveal him" (11: 27). Significantly, he ends his meditation with a fond reference to his heart: "Take my yoke upon you, and learn from me; for I am gentle and lowly in heart, and you will find rest for your souls" (11:29). The image of the welcoming savior is one of intimate revelation grounded ultimately in the experience of Alacoque, but now presented for everyone in clearly pastoral terms of comforting acceptance and support. The mystical revelation, couched in suffering and extreme experience, has become a universal message of consolation. The choice of the Sacred Heart of Jesus suits the occasion of a community celebrating and remembering the contributions of its spiritual shepherd, a pastor. Accordingly, the inscription on a monument in Gulpen indicates that the town erected the monument to recognize "its shepherd."[67] In 1949, the parish of St. Lambert in Helden dedicated a Sacred Heart statue "to its shepherd," Rev. Jaspers, where he had served since 1899. About the figure of Jesus are sheep, suggesting that the image of the Sacred Heart has been merged with the Good Shepherd.[68]

There are also several references to Christ as King (fig. 7). Some of the statues were consecrated on the Feast of Christ the King, held on the last Sunday of October, established by Pius XI in 1925. Although he mentioned the Sacred Heart only in passing in his encyclical, Pius XI made the connection firmly in a letter of 1928 discussing the "Reparation Due to the Sacred Heart."[69] The Feast of Christ the King celebrated the revelation of Christ's kingship during his interrogation by Pilate, when, asked if he is a king by the Roman leader, Jesus replies: "You say that I am a king. For this I was born, and for this I have come into the world, to bear witness to the truth" (John 18: 37). In the statues dedicated to Christ's kingship, Jesus points with one hand to the emblem of the Sacred Heart on his chest. He raises his other hand, the right one, in a gesture of benediction.[70] The reference to Christ's kingship is both biblical and liturgical. The inscription beneath the figure reads *"Rex Sum Ego. Joan. XVIII. Ik ben koning"* (I am King. John 18.) The Latin inscription quotes the Vulgate, John 18: 37: *"Tu dicis quia rex sum ego."* Once again, the theme allows for Jesus to dwell on the revelation that his life and especially his passion and death occasion. The gesture toward his heart indicates that the truth of his mission is encapsulated there. Some statues proclaim that the Sacred Heart of Jesus reigns over the town that has erected the figure.[71] The Christ as king motif is developed in a few statues in the familiar form of the liturgical prayer (Litany of the Sacred Heart) from the Latin: *Cor Jesu Rex et centrum omnium cordium misere nobis* – "Heart of Jesus, King in the center of all hearts, take pity on us."[72] The pastoral nature of the theme is signaled strongly in many inscriptions, especially the following, which combines two common themes, the welcoming savior of comfort and the king facing Roman interrogation and execution: "Come to me. I am king. The source of life and sanctity. The source of all solace."[73]

The regal presentation of Jesus was underscored by a ritual "enthronement" (*intronisatie*) that formally installed the statue in the community, and encouraged families of the parish to enthrone the Sacred Heart in their homes. The Chilean Jesuit Father Mateo Crawley-Boevy, principal promoter of the cause, was on hand to encourage the ceremony in Limburg.[74] In addition to remembering a priest or community member, the enthronement consecrated the community to the Sacred Heart of Jesus, and therefore expanded the capacity of the

Fig. 8. Thomas Kelly, "The Sacred Heart Consecration", 1874, lithograph. Courtesy Library of Congress.

image to serve as a sign or symbol. But Father Mateo's interest was focused on family consecrations, reviving a nineteenth-century campaign of enthroning an image or statue of the Sacred Heart in homes in a formal ceremony.[75] An American lithograph of 1874 (fig. 8) was one of many designed for use in the ritual of consecration and subsequent display in the home. Its appearance has been adapted to domestic use: the heart bears no gash and resembles a Valentine's heart more than the bodily organ it represents. Even the drops of blood appear as neatly ordered, shiny pearls rather than anything like gore. The image is framed within a decorative scheme that bears the floral motifs popular in chromolithography of the day. On the left appear the instruments of Christ's Passion and Crucifixion – the spear, hyssop sponge, hammer, and nails. To the left are lilies signifying the Resurrection. Each corner presents additional symbolic devices that allude to word

Fig. 9. Dutch catholic family in prayer before their home altar of the Sacred Heart, as drawn by Herman Moerkerk in 1925. Nijmegen KDC.

and sacrament, the cross, and the papal tiara and the powerful Office of the Keys (the Papacy's power to bind and release sin).

In 1915 Pope Benedict XV extended an indulgence to all families of the world for enthroning the image in their homes. The aim, which may be traced back to Alacoque, was to dedicate a religious or civic domain – community, diocese, municipality, county, or nation – to the Sacred Heart, thereby making public faith the better to effect reparations. The statue, like the Basilica of the Sacred Heart in Paris, stands forth as a public testimony, a visual proclamation of the dedication. The installation of the image was subsequently commemorated in homes with a ceremony prepared for families by the Director-General of the Apostleship of Prayer (which published *Messenger of the*

Sacred Heart of Jesus). The text, summarized by Fr. Bainvel, a historian of the Sacred Heart, combined "a profession of absolute submission to the teachings of the Church and to the directions of the Pope" with domestic observance of the devotion, including "the placing of the image of the Sacred Heart in a prominent position in the house" (fig. 9).[76]

Enthronement in the home corresponded to enthronement in the communal, civil, and universal life of the Church. The cloaked figure in several Dutch sculptures (fig. 10) stands atop a globular form, presumably as king of the universe, presenting his hands at either side for inspection of the wounds. The occasion for the creation of the monument shown in Fig. 10 was the culmination of a mission effort in 1921 undertaken by the parish of St. Nicholas in Broekhuizen, where the sculpture stands. The gesture of Christ appears to welcome those who responded to the invitation to attend worship and the inscription underscores the invitation. The devotion to the Sacred Heart is broadened in this iconography and used to represent the widest sense of Christ's love: the figure stands, as it were, at the entrance of the Church, beckoning all to enter under the blessing of comfort and reassurance. The sacramental significance of the wounds is directed to the compassion of Christ as redeemer and shepherd or sustainer of the flock. The figure type may be indebted to statuary from the Basilica of the Sacred Heart in Paris (see fig. 5).[77]

This is no longer the totem of a subculture within the Church, nor an insignia of a special vocation or movement within the church militant, but a very public signification of the most universal function of the savior. The highly formulaic sculptures, always presenting a very subdued and solemn demeanor, turn the more intimate engagement of the paintings and prints of the nineteenth century into a conventionalized format that speaks the visual language of official commemoration, the sedate visual language of remembrance, ceremonial occasion, communal consecration, and formulated meaning. Liturgical references frequently appear within the inscriptions and the formal gestures and symbolic devices within the figures' iconography assure the viewer that these are not the individualized works of artists, but

Fig. 10. J. Thissen, Roermond, "Sacred Heart", Church of St. Nicholas, Broekhuisen, Limburg, 1921. Photo: E. Geelen.

visual types that conform to widely-prescribed expectations and long-revered conventions. Their purpose is to bestow solemnity upon those they remember and to engage the community in hallowed acts of official memory. To be sure, there are instances of individual variation and artistic interpretation, and we know the names of many of the designers. But even then they bear many of the essential features of the pervasive formula: foot-length robes, spread arms, solemn demeanor, standing format, rigid and conventional gestures. Variations occur within the overall structure of the type so that the figure, whether innovative or not, will observe the principal function of speaking to the community in remembering one of its devoted members who performed the selfless love that enacted the exemplary love symbolized by the Sacred Heart of Jesus.

Finally, one of the most common of features among the statues is to arrange one or both of the hands of Christ to display their sacramental wounds. This occurs in at least one-fourth of the 105 examples collected by Godfried Egelie (fig. 10).[78] Clearly, this iconography remembers the close association of the Sacred Heart with the Eucharist and the Passion in the visions of Alacoque and in the practice and theology of the devotion ever since (in 1765 the Feast of the Sacred Heart was proclaimed by Clement XIII to take place on the first Friday following the festival of Corpus Christi). But by shifting to the public display of the wound, the statuary stresses the liturgical and pastoral significance of the Sacred Heart. The task seems to be to bring the devotion to the very heart of Christianity: the forgiveness of sin accomplished in the Passion and Crucifixion. This is not in essence at odds with the devotion's traditional dedication to penitential practices of paying reparations. Yet the emphasis on the symbolic nature of the Sacred Heart, as a symbol of divine love generally understood, seems to temper the private intensity of the devotion by steering it toward the public, liturgical practice of worship and community life.

5. Critique and Accommodation in the Twentieth Century

A series of encyclicals by modern popes from Leo XIII to Pius XII celebrated the Sacred Heart of Jesus as the devotion continued to enjoy popular support during the first half of the century. But there are several ways in which the devotion's iconography has been transcended and challenged, bringing this history to the present moment. The imagery has not been without its modern critics for reasons varying from theology to aesthetics. In 1958 the German Catholic theologian Richard Egenter published *Kitsch und Christenleben*, which was later translated into English as *The Desecration of Christ*, an unrelenting attack on "kitsch" in the Catholic Church. He included depictions of the Sacred Heart among the images he despised as tasteless and inimical to the faith. Egenter recalled a familiar theme when he lamented in a contemporary example of a Sacred Heart holy card "the incompatibility of realism and symbolism... the representation of a realistic heart on top of our Lord's clothes is immediately repugnant."[79] Egenter expressed further contempt for the presumption of placing Jesus and the human soul in parity, something visually coordinated in the conventional portrait iconography. The verse of a popular hymn to the Sacred Heart provided him with a lyrical instance:

> As thou art meek and lowly
> And ever pure of heart,
> So may my heart be wholly
> Of thine the counterpart.[80]

"In what way can my heart be a counterpart to God's?" Egenter demanded.

Even among some who remain devoted to the Sacred Heart today, the idea of a plainly displayed organ, or even the symbol of one, is objectionable since, as I was told in Kenya recently, "African Catholics see the image of Jesus in totality, they don't separate the heart from the person of Jesus."[81] Accordingly, a life-sized bronze sculpture of Jesus in the sanctuary of the Shrine of the Sacred Heart of Jesus in Karen, Kenya, a suburb of Nairobi, shows him referring to himself in a manner similar to the traditional iconography of the Sacred Heart, but with no heart visible on his chest (fig. 11). Even the stigmatum has been removed from his other hand, which extends outward in welcome. The devotion has shifted to "feeling close to Jesus, an emphasis on his kindliness, his love for his neighbor. The Sacred Heart means trust in God and how to live with suffering. The message is that Jesus suffers with you." My informant, Fr. Callisto Locheng, who is himself devoted to the Sacred Heart, told me that the devotion is promoted by parish priests more than by the Catholic hierarchy in Kenya. The pastoral nature of the devotion, especially in rural parishes in Kenya, seems clear, and the sculpture underscored the move from reparations and penance to the comforting presence of the divine friend. The sculpture was explicitly requested by Fr. John Marengoni. A Comboni missionary and co-founder of the Apostles of Jesus, Marengoni was the founder and designer of the shrine. He told the sculptor Vincenzo Gasparetti to create the figure without any heart since, according to Fr. Locheng, "people know what the heart means and do not need to have it designated because [they understand that] the heart refers to the whole person – both in general human experience and in the case of Jesus."[82] The irony is remarkable: for two centuries debate raged over whether the Heart split the person of Christ. Now devotees themselves have accepted the claim, resulting in the elimination of the heart.

The French Jesuit priest and paleontologist Pierre Teilhard de Chardin provides an apt place to end this historical account. His ideas gathered up the many oppositions noted in the history of the devotion and resolved many of them in a mystical vision of matter as a universal process of spiritual evolution. Teilhard recalled late in his life the childhood piety that his devout mother encouraged – the devotion to the Sacred Heart of Jesus. He remembered with a certain embarrassment the history of the piety beginning with Alacoque, how it was "oddly limited both in the object to which it was directed ('Reparations') and in its symbol (the heart of our Saviour, depicted with curiously anatomical realism!)."[83] The legacy of this dual set of imaginative limitations was evident to him: "The remains of this narrative view can still, unfortunately, be seen today, both in a form of worship obsessed with sin and in an iconography which we must needs deplore without too much vexation."

Although he claimed that at the time the devotions exerted not "the least attraction for my piety," a story that Teilhard fondly told suggests otherwise. In a fictional guise, he told of sitting in a church, wondering how Christ "would fit himself into Matter and so be sensibly apprehended."[84] As he contemplated the question, his eyes came to rest on a picture of Christ offering his Sacred Heart to humanity. As he gazed upon the image, its outlines began to melt: "The edge which divided Christ from the surrounding world was changing into

Fig. 11. Vincenzo Gasparetti, "Sacred Heart of Jesus", 1996, bronze, life size, Shrine of the Sacred Heart of Jesus, Karen, Kenya. Photo author.

a layer of vibration in which all distinct delimitation was lost."[85] Teilhard concentrated his sight on the heart in the image, thinking it was the source of the mysterious effect, but as he did so he found himself returning to the face of Christ, which "drew me and held me."[86] Gazing into the eyes, he felt their radiance become all-embracing, "an infinite depth of Life, enchanting and glowing."[87] The eyes returned his gaze with a sweetness and tenderness that reminded him of his mother and then "became in the next moment as full of passion and as dominating as those of a sovereign lady," perhaps the Virgin herself.[88]

The intermingling of Christ, Teilhard's own mother, and the Mother of Jesus in his experience of the portrait paralleled the material dissolution of the image into the ambient universe, conveying visually Teilhard's own view of the "Christified universe" or "amortized matter," which he described as "the great synthesis... of the Above with the Ahead."[89] Teilhard had come to regard the evolution of the material universe as producing the convergence of the divine and human, what he called the Universal Christ, the Ultra-Human, "a second species of Spirit," and "a sort of new God of the Ahead."[90] The future held the culmination of evolution, which would cancel the transcendence of the divine. In effect, evolution was resolving the dualism that critics had considered inherent in the Sacred Heart of Jesus – the uneasy relation of flesh and Divine Word. For Teilhard, his mother's piety was being transformed by a convergence of human and divine into a transfigured matter, or the "divine milieu." If this "religion of evolution" would not please many Catholics, especially those who objected to it as pantheism, which undermined the transcendence of God, it remains a conception that is friendly to evolutionary science, on the one hand, and a mystical sense of nature, on the other.[91] It remains a striking transfiguration of Alacoque's devotion, which had been fueled by pain and self-negation and a profound sense of sin that no amount of penance was able to eradicate. An altogether different spirit animated Teilhard's mysticism: an abiding sense of wonder that found the heart of matter impregnated with divinity and conveyed to him by the scintillating gaze of Jesus, or Mary, or both of them and his mother no less. It was not a gaze to suffer, but one to relish as an iconic disclosure of awesome mysteries to come.

Notes

1. For early opposition, see Alacoque's letter to her Jesuit ally and confessor, Father Jean Croiset, September 15, 1689, in *The Letters of St. Margaret Mary Alacoque*, tr. Clarence A. Herbst (Rockford, Ill.: TAN Books and Publishers, Inc., 1997), 214. A selection of her letters and her autobiography in the original French appear in Sainte Marguerite-Marie, *Oeuvres Choisies* (Paray-le-Monial: Monastère de la Visitation Sainte-Marie, 1962). A complete set of her writings is Marguerite-Marie Alacoque, *Vie et Oeuvres*, 2 vols. (Paris: Éditions Saint-Paul, 1990-93).
2. Letter of June 10, 1618. For a reproduction of the diagram as it appeared as the seal of the Convent of the Visitation at Paray-le-Monial, see A. Denizot, *Le Sacré-Coeur et la Grande Guerre* (Paris: Nouvelles Éditions Latines, 1994), 19.
3. Saint John Eudes, *The Sacred Heart of Jesus*, tr. Richard Flower (New York: P.J. Kennedy & Sons, 1946), 1.
4. Ibid., 7-8.
5. *The Autobiography of Saint Margaret Mary Alacoque*, tr. Sisters of the Visitation (Rockford, Ill.: TAN Books and Publishers, Inc., 1986), 106.
6. Alacoque, *Letters*, 168-69, #110, October 22, 1689.
7. Alacoque, *Autobiography*, 95; *Oeuvres Choisies*, 86: "...il me montra son sacré Coeur comme une ardente fournaise..." Eudes's *Sacred Heart of Jesus* appeared in 1681, the year following his death, as one of twelve books under the title *Le Coeur Admirable de la Très Sainte Mère de Dieu*.
8. Letter to Croiset, September 15, 1686, in Alacoque, *Letters*, 214, #132.
9. Ibid. In a letter of August 14, 1685, *Letters*, 47, #35, Alacoque mentioned that a male visitor to the convent learned of the image through one of the novices, presumably a family member, and pledged himself to securing a painted version of it. We learn in a letter of March 20, 1686, however, that the Mother Superior at Paray-le-Monial refused to allow plans to proceed because she "wants our community to have a chapel built later on, in which is to be placed a beautiful picture of this Sacred Heart," Alacoque, *Letters*, 58, #44.
10. Letter of November 3, 1689, to Croiset, in Alacoque, *Letters*, 229.
11. The English translation is inaccurate, referring to the image as "a small ink etching representing the Divine Heart," *Autobiography*, 108. In fact, the French states that the image was a pen-and-ink drawing: "Ce qu'elles firent de bon Coeur, en faisant un petit autel, sur lequel elles

mirent un[e] petit[e] image de papier crayonné avec une plume," *Oeuvres Choisies*, 99. The "plume" or feather and the verb "crayonner," to draw, could not mean "etching." Moreover, engravings of the image did not appear until 1688, as Alacoque's correspondence with Mother de Saumise in 1686-1688 clearly shows – see her letter to Mother de Saumise, January 17, 1688, #79 (*Letters*, 109).

12. Alacoque acknowledged the first gift of an image in a letter dated January 1686 to Pérrone-Rosalie Greyfié, mother superior of the Visitationist convent in Semur, *Letters*, 52, #39.
13. For other early mentions of pictures and their production, see Alacoque, *Letters*, 52, 54, 57-8, 61-2, 64, 68, 70, 72, 109, 151.
14. Ibid., 50, #36.
15. Ibid., 72, #52.
16. Ibid., 53.
17. Ibid., 58.
18. Ibid., 229.
19. Ibid., 70; 193.
20. Ibid., 230, #133, November 3, 1689.
21. In 1686, Alacoque reported hearing a voice that told her the infidel Huguenots would have been converted if the father in question had fulfilled his promise to get the image engraved, letter of April 23, 1686, #46, *Letters*, 61; see also p. 193.
22. The history of Jansenist ideas, politics, and the many controversies among Jesuits and Jansenists across Europe from the seventeenth century even to its persistent memory in the nineteenth century, long after efforts at Jansenist reform had ended, have received consideration attention among historians. For a good introduction, see John McManners, *Church and Society in Eighteenth-century France*, 2 vols. (Oxford: Clarendon Press, 1998), esp. vol. 2, 345-69.
23. Dale K. Van Kley, *The Religious Origins of the French Revolution: From Calvin to the Civil Constitution, 1560-1791* (New Haven: Yale University Press, 1996), 117.
24. Joseph de Gallifet, *De cultu Sacrosancti Cordis Dei ac Domini nostri Jesus Christi* (Rome: apud Joannem Mariam Salviorii, 1726). The first French edition was *L'excellence de la devotion au Coeur adorable de Jésus-Christ* (Nancy: Veuve Baltasard, 1733). Father Joseph de Gallifet, *The Adorable Heart of Jesus* (Philadelphia: Messenger of the Sacred Heart, 1890) is an English translation of the third French edition (Nancy, 1745).
25. Alacoque, *Letters*, 65.

26. Gallifet, *The Adorable Heart of Jesus*, 23. See Raymond Jonas, *France and the Cult of the Sacred Heart: An Epic Tale for Modern Times* (Berkeley: University of California Press, 2000), 34-53, for the case of Marseilles in the history of the devotion.
27. Ibid., 44.
28. Alphonsus de Liguori, *Novena to the Sacred Heart*, tr. Frederick M. Jones, in *Selected Writings*, ed. Frederick M. Jones (New York: Paulist Press, 1999), 223.
29. Jon L. Seydl, "Contesting the Sacred Heart of Jesus in Late Eighteenth-century Rome," in Andrew Hopkins and Maria Wyke, eds., *Roman Bodies: Antiquity to the Eighteenth Century* (London: The British School at Rome, 2005), 215.
30. Ibid., 218. For further historical discussion of Batoni's image, see the helpful study by Christopher M. S. Johns, "That Amiable Object of Adoration': Pompeo Batoni and the Sacred Heart," *Gazette des Beaux-Arts* 132, nos. 1554-55 (July-August 1998): 19-28.
31. A very instructive study in English of Ricci's career and thought is Charles A. Bolton, *Church Reform in 18th Century Italy (The Synod of Pistoia, 1786)* (The Hague: Martinus Nijhoff, 1969); for a discussion of the occasion of the riot see 118-19.
32. Ibid., 121.
33. Quoted in ibid, 10-11. Emphasis added.
34. Pius VI, "Errors of the Synod of Pistoia," in *Auctorem fidei*, August 28, 1794; reprinted in Heinrich Joseph Dominik Denziger, *The Sources of Catholic Dogma*, tr. Roy J. Deferrari from the Thirtieth Edition of Henry Denzinger's *Enchiridion Symbolorum* (St. Louis: B. Herder Book Co., 1957), 383.
35. Ibid.
36. Ibid., 389.
37. Margaret Williams, R.S.C.J., *St. Madeleine Sophie: Her Life and Letters* (New York: Herder and Herder, 1965), 201, 301, 348, 593.
38. Quoted in ibid, 197-98.
39. Ibid., 502.
40. Rev. Peter J. Arnoudt, SJ, *The Imitation of the Sacred Heart of Jesus* (New York: Benziger Brothers, 1904; reprint, Rockford, Illinois: TAN Books and Publishers, Inc., 2001), 117.
41. Ibid., 51.
42. Williams, *St. Madeleine Sophie*, 528.
43. Thomas B. Noonan & Co. was a publishing firm in Boston that specialized in Catholic materials, operating from 1850 to 1900.

44. An exhibition displayed at the Visitationist house in Paray-le-Monial (Alacoque's own convent), entitled "Exposition sur l'histoire et l'actualité de la dévotion au Sacré-Coeur de Jésus," viewable online at http://www.spiritualite-chretienne.com/exposition/Sacre-Coeur.html, gathered several hundred prints, medals, scapulars, pendants, and devotional cards dating from around 1700 to the present. Perhaps a dozen showing Jesus with the Sacred Heart dated before 1850, some clearly indebted to Batoni, others less so. The decisive point in the portrait-style image was the mid-nineteenth century.
45. Reproduced in Jonas, *France and the Cult of the Sacred Heart*, 152. Épinal is synonymous with mass-produced print imagery in France because it was where the production of inexpensive wood-cuts began in 1796 with a firm established by Jean-Charles Pellerin, which produced many religious motifs. See Jean-Marie Dumont, *Les maîtres graveurs populaires 1800-1850* (Épinal: Imagerie Pellerin, 1965).
46. Jonas, *France and the Cult of the Sacred Heart*, 9-33.
47. Auguste Hamon, *Histoire de la Dévotion au Sacré Coeur*, 5 vols. (Paris: Gabriel Beauchesne, 1923), 4: 307. Hamon spoke of the "prêtre non assermenté," referring to priests who did not swear allegiance to the Revolutionary government's Civil Constitution in order to serve as official clergy.
48. A comprehensive and beautifully illustrated treatment of the basilica's history is Jacques Benoist, ed., *Le Sacré-Coeur de Montmartre: Un Voeu National* (Paris: Délégation à l'action artistique de la ville de Paris, 1995).
49. I have considered the difference between empathy and sympathy in eighteenth and nineteenth-century popular visual practice in *Visual Piety: A History and Theory of Popular Religious Images* (Berkeley: University of California Press, 1998), 59-96.
50. His remarks originally appeared in *Brownson's Quarterly Review* 23 (July 1874), 421-424. They were reprinted in *The Works of Orestes A. Brownson*, ed. Henry F. Brownson, 20 vols. (Detroit: H. F. Brownson, 1887), 20: 418-20. The quoted passage appears on p. 420.
51. Anonymous letter, signed "Not a Jesuit," reprinted in *Works*, 20: 414.
52. Letter to the Editor, signed "A Jesuit and a Friend," reprinted in *Works*, 20: 422-23.
53. "Hymn of Reparation," *Messenger*, n.s. 2, no. 7 (July 1875): 295.
54. The Dutch version was published in 1870 by Fr. R. Pierik, S.J. at Bois-le-Duc. The English translation in *Messenger* was re-published in the United States under Pierik's name in 1874 (Baltimore: J. Murphy).

55. "Catechism of the Devotion to the Heart of Jesus," *Messenger* 7, no. 5 (May 1872): 212.
56. Ibid., 213.
57. Ibid., 214.
58. Ibid., 214. Italics in original.
59. "Catechism of the Devotion to the Heart of Jesus," *Messenger* 7, no. 7 (July 1872): 311.
60. Ibid., 313.
61. "Sympathy with Jesus," *Messenger*, n.s. 1, no. 6 (June 1874): 255-64.
62. Ibid., 258.
63. Ibid., 263.
64. Alacoque, *Letters*, 98.
65. "Montmartre: A Pilgrimage to the Shrine of the 'National Vow,'" *Messenger*, n.s. 5, no. 10 (October 1890): 732. The sculpture may be the plaster figure produced by Georges Thomas; see note 77 below.
66. Godfried C.M. Egelie, *Beeld van het Heilig Hart in Limburg: Religieuze en Sociale Betekenis van de Verering in de Twintigste Eeuw* (Zutphen, Netherlands: Walburg Pers, 2004).
67. Ibid., 118.
68. Ibid., 123.
69. Pius XI, *Quas Primas*, December 11, 1925; Pius XI, *Miserentissimus Redemptor*, May 8, 1928; translated as *The Reparation Due to the Sacred Heart*, tr. Msgr. James H. Ryan (New York: America Press, 1928).
70. Egelie, *Beeld van het Heilig Hart in Limburg*, see fig. on p. 120; also pp. 96, 100, 129, 138, 152, 155, 161, 164, 178, 186.
71. Ibid., 178. Several statues portraying Christ the King do not show him pointing to his heart, but spreading his arms wide as if presenting himself for homage to the viewer (see pp. 101, 107, 131, 159, 163, 165, 176,), or holding one aloft in an imperial gesture that ultimately derives from standing portraits of Roman Caesars (pp. 132, 142, 151, 154). The triumphal character, which recalls the monumental mosaic portraying the "Triomphe de Sacré Coeur" in the apse of the Basilica of the Sacred Heart on Montmartre (see Benoist, ed., *Le Sacré-Coeur de Montmartre*, 185), signals the Church's assertion of Jesus in a twentieth-century world buffeted by unbelief and war.
72. Egelie, *Beeld van het Heilig Hart in Limburg*, 176, 138, 100.
73. Ibid., 101.
74. Egelie discusses Father Mateo and the enthronement rite, ibid., 20-24.

75. For a discussion of this see J. V. Bainvel, *Devotion to the Sacred Heart of Jesus: The Doctrine and Its History*, tr. E. Leahy, ed. Rev. George O'Neill (New York: Benziger Brothers, [1924]), 328-33. The movement, though focused on homes, made use of churches to disseminate the ritual to families. See *Proceedings of the First National Congress of the Enthronement of the Sacred Heart in the Home* (Washington, D.C.: National Center of the Enthronement, 1946).
76. Bainvel, *Devotion to the Sacred Heart*, 330.
77. About 1890, Georges Thomas produced his plaster model of a standing Christ, with arms outstretched, somewhat like the figure reproduced in *The Messenger* in 1890 (see fig. 6). Thomas had been commissioned to create the figure for the central niche of the principal façade of the Basilica. But the sculpture was accidentally destroyed and replaced with the work of another sculptor, Gustave Michel, about 1900. Michel's figure does not stand on the Heart, but draws aside his mantle with one hand to display the Heart on his chest. See Veronique Gautherin, "Mémoire d'une sculpture oubliée," in Benoist, ed., *Le Sacré-Coeur de Montmartre*, 172. Thomas's figure appears on p. 175; Michel's sculpture is reproduced on p. 233.
78. Examples are found in Egelie, *Beeld van het Heilig Hart in Limburg*, pp. 90, 100, 101, 107, 109, 110, 112, 117, 122, 123, 128, 132, 134, 136, 142, 143, 149, 153, 162, 165, 168.
79. Richard Egenter, *The Desecration of Christ*, tr. Edward Quinn, ed. Nicolete Gray (Chicago: Franciscan Herald Press, 1967), 48.
80. Ibid., 100.
81. Father Callisto Locheng, Dean, Faculty of Arts and Social Sciences, Catholic University of Eastern Africa, Karen, Kenya. Interview with the author, August 8, 2007.
82. Ibid.
83. Pierre Teilhard de Chardin, *The Heart of Matter*, tr. René Hague (New York: Harcourt Brace Jovanovich, 1976), 43.
84. Ibid., 62. The account first appeared in Pierre Teilhard de Chardin, *Hymn of the Universe*, tr. Simon Bartholomew (New York: Harper & Row, 1965), where an editorial note indicates that though the stories are related in the third person, the individual in the story is Teilhard himself, p. 41.
85. Teilhard, *The Heart of Matter*, 62-3.
86. Ibid., 64.
87. Ibid., 65.
88. Ibid.

89. Ibid., 44.
90. Ibid., 45.
91. For his endorsement of "a religion of evolution," see ibid., 97.